MOLLY
Gets Her Wheels

Written by Sherry Carnahan

Art Direction by Tammie Lyon   Illustration by Laura Merer

Published by FlyHigh Media, LLC.

This book is dedicated to Molly and special needs animals everywhere. Our house has always been filled with 'misfit' animals and we wouldn't have it any other way. Not only do they have so much love to give but their spirit to persevere when faced with challenges is awe inspiring and can't help but touch your heart! They are very "special" indeed.

I also want to give a huge THANK YOU to my very talented artists Laura Merer and Tammie Lyon. Without them, this story would be in words only and still tucked inside a drawer or computer file. Together, they helped me bring Molly's story to life and to the world. I am forever grateful!!

Visit my website to learn more about Molly and download fun activity and coloring pages.
www.sherrycarnahan.com/molly

With Love,

Sherry

Molly Gets Her Wheels

Copyright © 2019 by Sherry Carnahan www.sherrycarnahan.com
Illustrations by Laura Merer www.lauramerer.com
Art Direction by Tammie Lyon www.tammielyon.com
Cover and page Layout by Phil Ulrich www.designbyinsight.net

For permission requests, email the publisher, Subject line: "Attention: Permissions Coordinator" at the address below.
Fly High Media, LLC.
Office@flyhighmediallc.com

ATTN: Animal Shelters and Rescues:
Special discounts are available on quantity purchases of this book for the purpose of fundraising by your organization. For details, contact our sales department by emailing: office@flyhighmediallc.com

Molly Gets Her Wheels / Sherry Carnahan -- 1st ed.

This book is cataloged with the Library of Congress.

Hard Copy: ISBN-13: 978-0-9600527-0-7 | ISBN-10: 0-9600527-0-4
Ebook: ISBN-13: 978-0-9600527-1-4 | ISBN-10: 0-9600527-1-2
Paperback: ISBN-13: 978-0-9600527-2-1 | ISBN-10: 0-9600527-2-0

On a lazy summer day on the deck high above the backyard of her house, Molly and her brother Jake were napping happily in the sun.

FTH-FTH-FTH, F-F-F-F!
Molly's ears perked up, followed quickly by her head.

Her eyes opened wide.

A big black and white dog was digging in their flower garden!
"Who are you and why are you digging in our yard?"
Molly barked angrily.

"Get out of our yard!" growled Jake.

But the dog just kept digging, totally
ignoring anything Molly and Jake
had to say.

"I told you to leave!" Molly barked harshly. She began to wiggle through the railing on the deck. "I really mean it!"

Jake watched helplessly as Molly, with one final push, sailed all the way through the railing.

With a loud *"CRASH"*, Molly found herself lying on the patio below. Startled, the black and white dog scampered away as fast as he could.

Jake rushed to Molly's side.

"I don't think I can move!" she cried.

"This must be really bad," thought Molly
as she lay in the backseat of the car
on the way to see the vet, Dr. Mike.

She knew her family would care for her
the best that they could.

When the X-rays came back, it was clear there was a problem.

"I'm afraid Molly has broken a bone in her back," said Dr. Mike.
"I'm not sure she will ever be able to run and play again. I'm very sorry."

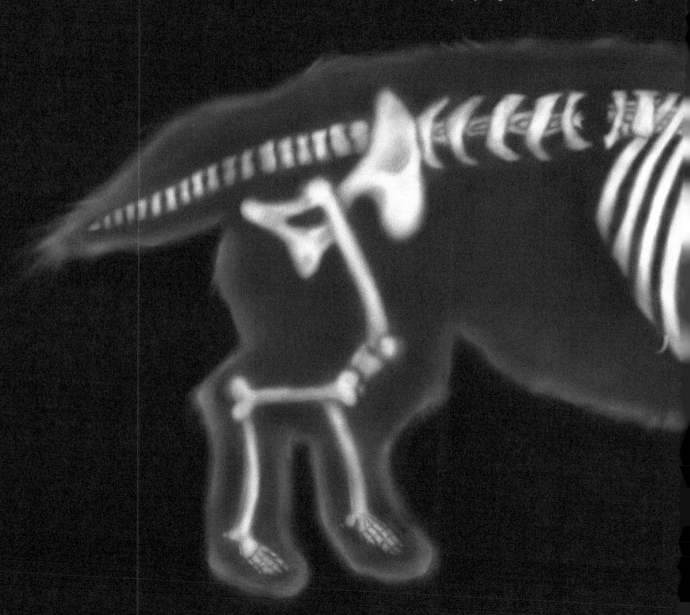

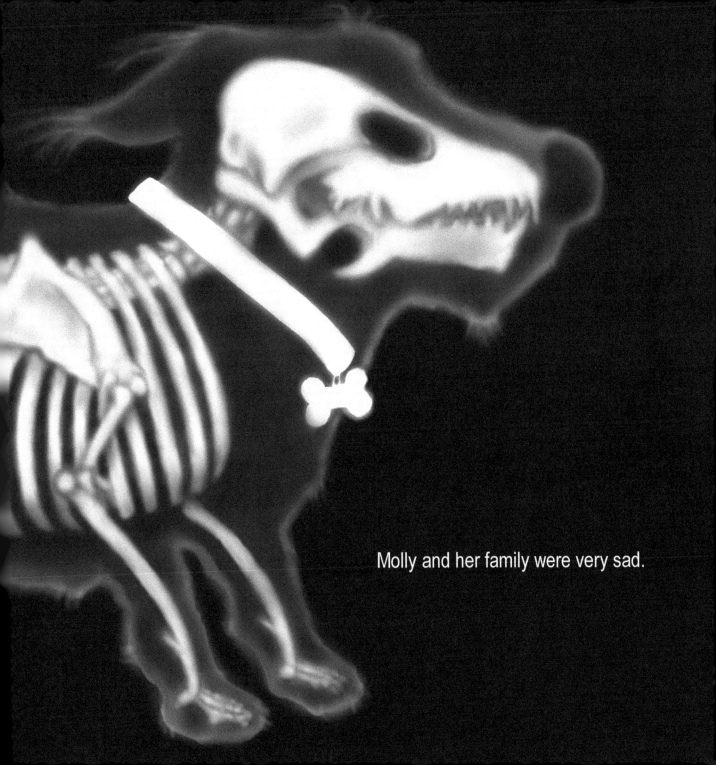

Molly and her family were very sad.

When they went back home, Jake tried to get Molly to chase the squirrels in the backyard.

She tried but had no luck.

"I don't think I'll ever be able to chase squirrels again,"
she told Jake.

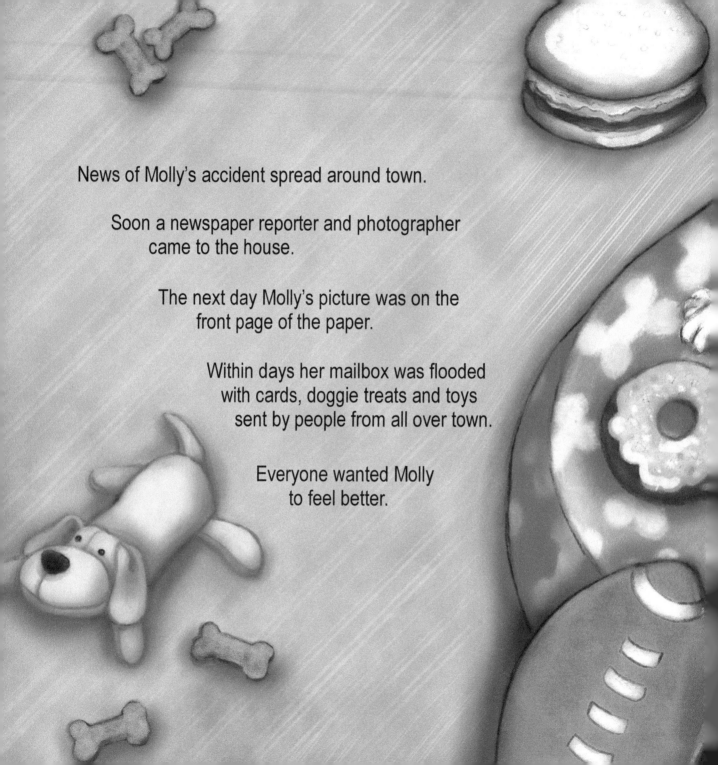

News of Molly's accident spread around town.

Soon a newspaper reporter and photographer
came to the house.

The next day Molly's picture was on the
front page of the paper.

Within days her mailbox was flooded
with cards, doggie treats and toys
sent by people from all over town.

Everyone wanted Molly
to feel better.

"I love my new toys and treats," Molly told Jake
as they lay together in the grass.

"But I still can't run and play."

Jake whispered into Molly's ear,
"It will be alright. I know our family
will think of something."

Just then the family came around the corner with
the biggest red wagon Molly had ever seen.

The family put Molly inside, and before she knew it,
she was rolling down the street, with Jake trotting alongside.

"Wheeeee!!!!!"

They went to the park where Molly said
"Hello" to Angel, her best friend.

Then she had ice cream
at her favorite ice cream stand.

"This is great!" Molly said to Jake

"But I still wish I could run
and chase squirrels
like we used to."

Later that week there was a knock at the door. Jake ran while Molly scooted to see who it might be.

When the door opened there was a lady named Amy and her dog Ace standing there.

Only Ace wasn't standing like a normal dog.

"What is that?" barked Molly. She scurried to get a closer look at him.

"These are my wheels," Ace said proudly.

"Wheels?" asked Molly.

"Yep, wheels. I had an accident too and my owners found this special wheelchair made just for dogs.Now I can run and play like I always have."

Molly and Jake checked out the wheelchair.
It had a big strap in the front like a collar.

In the back it had two wheels with black loops
that were perfect for a dog's back legs to rest in.

"Oh Ace, I wish I had one of these!" barked Molly excitedly.

Just then she heard Amy talking to her family.

"We heard of Molly's story and since Ace has a couple of extra wheelchairs, we wanted to give one to Molly."
Molly's ears perked up.

"A wheelchair for me?" she thought excitedly.

Amy sat two wheelchairs down on the floor.

"I'm sure one of these will fit her just perfectly."

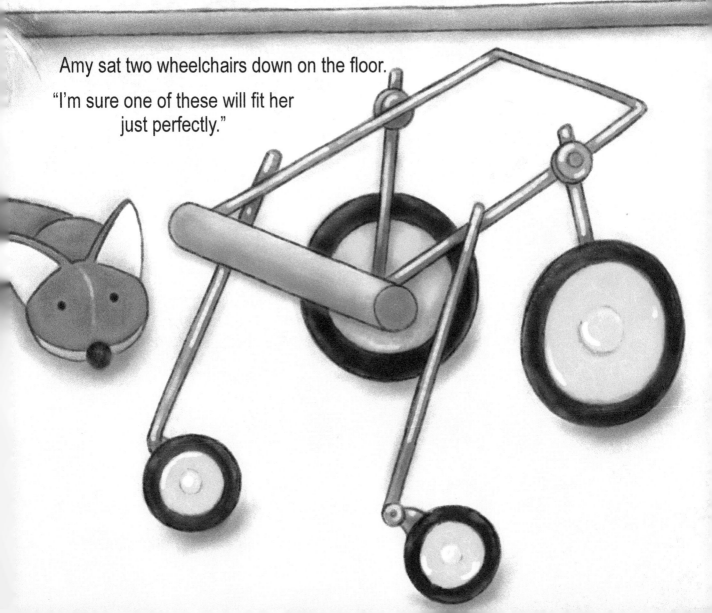

Molly squealed with delight as her family lifted her into a wheelchair.

At first she didn't know what to do.
When she started to move her front paws, she went backwards.

"Look out!" barked Jake.

Molly couldn't see where she was going and ran into everything.

Then with a little help from her family, Molly took one bold step forward, then another...and another!

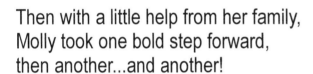

Soon she stepped faster and faster.

"Molly's walking again!" cheered her family.

They hurriedly opened the door to let Molly try out her new wheels.

With her head held high and a huge "doggie grin,"
Molly bolted out the door and into the sunshine with Jake fast on her heels.

"Let's go get Angel!" barked Molly.

Soon the three of them were playing in the backyard.

"I can chase the squirrels again!" barked Molly.

"Catch me if you can!" barked Jake
as he bounced around the yard.

They ran back and forth across the yard
as fast as they could.

"Yippeeee! Look at me! I can run again!" shouted Molly.

The next day when Molly trotted happily outside
to fetch the newspaper for her family,
she didn't even notice the headline.
In big bold letters it read:

"MOLLY GETS HER WHEELS!"

Laura Merer – Illustrator

Artist and Illustrator, Laura Merer, lives in California with her husband Adam and three teenage children, Aidan, Kyra, and Olivia. (She is also the loving owner of two dogs and a growing number of cats!)

Laura has illustrated several children books, including titles such as Santa Claus Is Coming To Town, Take Me Out To The Ball Game, Fuzzy Ducky's Birthday, and Where's Daddy?

When not drawing in her "Cow Cat Studio," Laura can be found working with kitten rescues, listening to podcasts, and watching Bob's Burgers (which she is addicted to)!

You can follow Laura on Instagram @lauramerer or visit her website at:
www.lauramerer.com

Tammie Lyon – Art Director

Award-winning author and illustrator, Tammie Lyon, lives in Ohio with her husband, Lee, and her dogs, Amos, Dudley, and Artie.

As an only child, drawing became a favorite form of self-entertainment. Beginning at a very young age, while drawing at the kitchen table with her dad, she would sit for hours drawing things around the house, later presenting them as gifts to her mother.

Today, she shares her gift with the world by illustrating books (well over 100!), posters, magazines, CDs, games, clothing—and just about anything else you can think of. She's even authored her first children's book, Olive and Snowflake (Marshall Cavendish). She is represented by MB Artists.

You can follow Tammie on Instagram @tammielyon or visit her website at:
www.tammielyon.com

CPSIA information can be obtained
at www.ICGtesting.com
Printed in the USA
LVHW072359041119
636252LV00013B/3075/P